Celebrations in My World

Valentine's Day

Reagan Miller

Crabtree Publishing Company

www.crabtreebooks.com

Crabtree Publishing Company
www.crabtreebooks.com

Author: Reagan Miller
Coordinating editor: Chester Fisher
Series and project editor: Penny Dowdy
Editor: Adrianna Morganelli
Proofreader: Crystal Sikkens
Editorial director: Kathy Middleton
Production coordinator: Katherine Berti
Prepress technician: Katherine Berti
Project manager: Kumar Kunal (Q2AMEDIA)
Art direction: Dibakar Acharjee (Q2AMEDIA)
Cover design: Tarang Saggar (Q2AMEDIA)
Design: Neha Kaul (Q2AMEDIA)
Photo research: Farheen Aadil (Q2AMEDIA)

Photographs:
123RF: Veniamin Kraskov: p. 19
Associated Press: p. 28
Dreamstime: p. 5
Fotolia: Petra Bihlmaier: p. 17
Getty Images: De Agostini Picture Library: p. 10; William Hart/Stone:
    p. 25; Giovanni Paolo Pannini/The Bridgeman Art Library: p. 7
Istockphoto: R. van der Beek: p. 24; Karen Hogan: front cover (foreground);
    Todd Media: p. 22 (top)
Jupiter Images: David Johnston: p. 23; Jose Luis Pelaez: p. 16 (top)
Photolibrary: Chuck Carlton: p. 27; North Wind Pictures: p. 9, 11
Photostogo: p. 14
Shutterstock: p. 12, 21, 26; Marilyn Barbone: p. 29; bhathaway:
    p. 22 (bottom); Marc Dietrich: p. 15 (computer); Pavel Eltsov:
    front cover (background); Kevin H. Knuth: p. 20; Maxstockphoto:
    p. 8; Lorelyn Medina: p. 16 (bottom); Monkey Business Images: p. 1;
    Oculo: p. 4; Dianka Pyzhova: p. 15 (cards); Victorian Traditions: p. 18

Library and Archives Canada Cataloguing in Publication

Miller, Reagan
    Valentine's Day / Reagan Miller.

(Celebrations in my world)
Includes index.
ISBN 978-0-7787-4759-8 (bound).--ISBN 978-0-7787-4777-2 (pbk.)

    1. Valentine's Day--Juvenile literature.
I. Title. II. Series: Celebrations in my world

GT4925.M54 2010   j394.2618   C2009-902388-1

Library of Congress Cataloging-in-Publication Data

Miller, Reagan.
    Valentine's Day / Reagan Miller.
        p. cm. -- (Celebrations in my world)
    Includes index.
    ISBN 978-0-7787-4777-2 (pbk. : alk. paper) -- ISBN 978-0-7787-4759-8
(reinforced library binding : alk. paper)
    1. Valentine's Day--Juvenile literature. I. Title. II. Series.

    GT4925.M55 2010
    394.2618--dc22
                                        2009016264

Crabtree Publishing Company
www.crabtreebooks.com   1-800-387-7650

Published in Canada
Crabtree Publishing
616 Welland Ave.
St. Catharines, ON
L2M 5V6

Published in the United States
Crabtree Publishing
PMB16A
350 Fifth Ave., Suite 3308
New York, NY 10118

Published in the United Kingdom
Crabtree Publishing
White Cross Mills
High Town, Lancaster
LA1 4XS

Published in Australia
Crabtree Publishing
386 Mt. Alexander Rd.
Ascot Vale (Melbourne)
VIC 3032

Contents

What is Valentine's Day? **4**

Holiday History **6**

Saint Valentine **8**

The Holiday Grows **10**

The First Valentines **12**

Be My Valentine **14**

Have a Heart! **16**

Cupid **18**

Lovebirds **20**

Giving Gifts **22**

Let's Celebrate! **24**

Spread the Love! **26**

Celebrations Around the World **28**

Words from the Heart **30**

Glossary and Index **32**

What is Valentine's Day?

FEB
14

Valentine's Day is a special day. People celebrate Valentine's Day every year on February 14. On this day, people honor friendship and love. It is a day to let family and friends know how special they are to you.

● Look at a calendar. On which day of the week is Valentine's Day this year?

DID YOU KNOW?

*Valentine's Day is not a **federal** holiday. Unlike many holidays, people do not close schools, banks, and government offices on Valentine's Day.*

4

On Valentine's Day, we can spend time with the people we love.

People first started celebrating Valentine's Day hundreds of years ago. Today, many countries around the world celebrate Valentine's Day. It is a day filled with love!

5

Holiday History

People think Valentine's Day began as a **festival** celebrated in **ancient** Rome. People celebrated the festival, called Lupercalia, every year on February 15. It was named after the Roman god Lupercus, who was the god of shepherds. On the night before the festival, every boy would draw a girl's name out of a vase. The girl would then become the boy's partner for the festival. Sometimes, the boy and girl fell in love and later got married.

DID YOU KNOW?

In ancient Rome, February 15 was the first day of spring. Lupercalia celebrated birth and the start of the new season.

Ancient Romans celebrated Lupercalia on the first day of spring.

Saint Valentine

Valentine's Day is named after a priest named Valentine. Long ago, a man named Claudius ruled over Rome. Claudius wanted to build an army. He believed married men would not leave their families to go fight in a war. To stop that from happening, Claudius made a law that said that young men could not get married.

From your Valentine

- People think Valentine once signed a letter to a friend "From your Valentine."

DID YOU KNOW?

People believe Valentine wrote a letter to a friend. He signed the letter "From your Valentine." Today, we write these words on Valentine's Day cards.

On Valentine's Day, we honor Saint Valentine's belief in love.

Valentine thought this rule was unfair. He disobeyed Claudius and secretly carried out marriage ceremonies for young couples. Claudius found out and had Valentine put to death. Valentine died on February 14.

9

The Holiday Grows

For many years, Valentine's Day was celebrated only in Rome. Then the Roman government sent its armies to other countries. Rome started wars to try to gain more land.

Rome wanted to gain control of other countries, such as England and France.

DID YOU KNOW?

*In the 1700s, people from Europe moved to North America. Europeans brought their holidays and **traditions** with them. This is how Valentine's Day started in North America.*

Roman soldiers fought to get control of France and England. They brought Roman holidays with them to these countries.

The soldiers continued to celebrate their Roman holidays while they were fighting in other countries. People living in these countries learned about Valentine's Day from the Roman soldiers. This is how holidays such as Valentine's Day began to be celebrated around the world.

The First Valentines

In the 1400s, people started sending Valentine's Day cards. Those cards looked very different from the ones we send today. **Rebus** cards used both pictures and words to write messages. For example, a picture of an eye would take the place of the word "I."

This rebus card says, "I love you! Will you be mine?"

DID YOU KNOW?

A British Museum has a Valentine's Day card from the year 1415.

When you unfold the puzzik card, you can read the message. This one says "For my sweet Valentine."

Puzzik cards were made from folded paper. There were messages written inside each of the folds. A person had to unfold the card in the correct order to read the message inside.

Be My Valentine

Today, many people buy Valentine's Day cards from stores. Some cards have funny jokes or stickers inside. Other cards even play music!

Giving someone a Valentine's Day card will bring a smile to his or her face!

#1 Dad

DID YOU KNOW?

Valentine's Day is a busy day for letter carriers. Each year, around one billion people mail Valentine's Day cards around the world!

People send Valentine's Day cards to family, friends, teachers, and even pets! Some people send "**virtual** valentines" using computers. E-cards are made on a computer and then sent by e-mail. E-cards are fun to make and also good for the environment since no paper is used to make them.

Many fun web sites can help you make an e-card!

Have a Heart!

There are different Valentine's Day **symbols**. Hearts are the most well-known Valentine's Day symbols. Long ago, people thought good feelings such as love and happiness came from our hearts.

People decorate valentines with hearts. Hearts stand for love!

DID YOU KNOW?

The hand on the left shows how to say "I love you" using American Sign Language.

These heart-shaped balloons are being released on Valentine's Day.

Since our real hearts are red, this color is used on Valentine's Day cards and decorations. Many people wear red clothing on Valentine's Day. Gift boxes and bags come in heart shapes or are decorated with hearts.

Cupid

Cupid is another Valentine's Day symbol. He is usually shown as a young boy with wings. Cupid carries a bow and arrow.

To my Valentine

In some stories, writers describe Cupid as playful and full of mischief.

DID YOU KNOW?

In ancient Roman stories, Cupid is the son of Venus, the goddess of love.

Long ago, the people of Rome believed Cupid was a god of love. In old stories, Cupid flew through the air shooting people with his magical arrows. The arrows did not hurt people, but made them fall in love with the person standing closest to them.

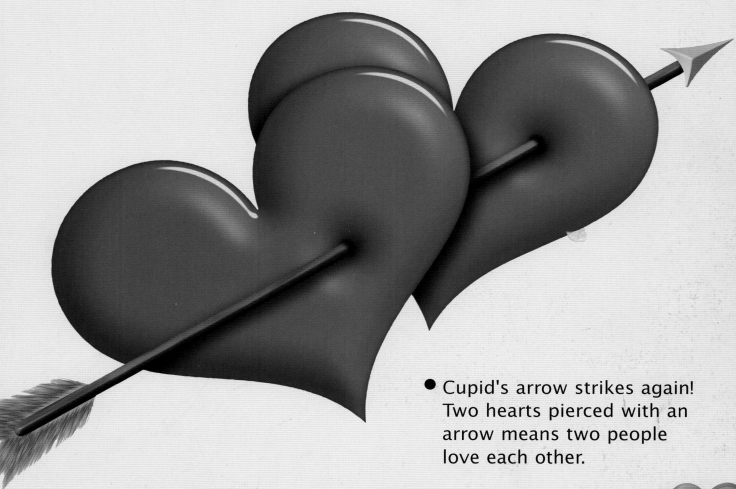

- Cupid's arrow strikes again! Two hearts pierced with an arrow means two people love each other.

Lovebirds

Lovebirds are another symbol of Valentine's Day. Lovebirds stand for love and **loyalty**.

A lovebird does not travel far from its mate. They often cuddle with one another.

DID YOU KNOW?

Two people who are very happy together are often called "lovebirds."

People of all ages celebrate Valentine's Day. These two are loyal "lovebirds!"

Long ago, many people believed that birds chose their mates, or partners, on February 14. They felt people should also find a partner to love on this day. Lovebirds got their name because they always stay close to their mates, just as people in love stay close to one another.

21

Giving Gifts

Some people give gifts, such as flowers and candy, on Valentine's Day. Red roses are the most popular flowers on Valentine's Day. Red roses are a symbol of love and beauty.

Valentine's Day has flower power! Florists sell over 50 million roses each Valentine's Day.

DID YOU KNOW?

More than 36 million heart-shaped boxes of chocolates are sold each Valentine's Day. The boxes are often decorated with satin and lace.

You can bake sweet treats, such as heart-shaped cookies, to give to friends and family.

You can also make Valentine's Day gifts. A gift you make yourself can be very special. A homemade gift or card has meaning and shows that you care.

Let's Celebrate!

People celebrate Valentine's Day in different ways. Sometimes children have Valentine's Day parties in their classrooms at school. Children might decorate their classroom, make Valentine's Day crafts, and eat treats!

● Can you see the heart shape inside this strawberry?

DID YOU KNOW?

Too many Valentine's Day sweets can make you sick! Strawberries are a healthy Valentine's Day treat. A strawberry cut in half looks like a little heart.

Some classes decorate a large box. The children can put their Valentine's Day cards inside the box until it is time to deliver the cards. Students also make their own special mailboxes to hang from their desks.

These children put Valentine's Day cards for classmates inside the special Valentine's Day mailbox.

Spread the Love!

Valentine's Day is a day to think about others. Remembering others is one way you can make Valentine's Day a wonderful day for everyone.

You do not need to wait for February 14. Celebrate love and friendship every day of the year!

DID YOU KNOW?

You do not have to wait for Valentine's Day to show you care. Tell people how much they mean to you every day!

You could make a card for someone who works hard in your **community**, such as a crossing guard or bus driver. You and your friends could make a big Valentine's Day card and send it to a children's hospital or **retirement home**. The person who reads your card will feel happy, and you will too.

Spread some Valentine's Day joy to the people in your community!

Celebrations Around the World

Today, many countries around the world celebrate Valentine's Day, including the United States, Canada, India, England, France, China, and Japan. Some places have special ways of celebrating the holiday.

A car in China is decorated with strawberries and chocolate for Valentine's Day.

In England, children go door-to-door singing Valentine's Day songs. In Wales, people decorate wooden love spoons to give to family and friends. In Denmark, people often send white flowers called "snowdrops" to their family and friends.

● Wooden love spoons, such as this one, have hearts, flowers, or other decorations.

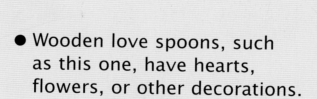

DID YOU KNOW?

"I love you" can be said in many languages.
"Je t'adore" means I love you in French.
"Te amo" means I love you in Spanish.

29

Words from the Heart

Long ago, people made acrostic Valentine's Day cards. An acrostic card uses each letter in a person's name to write something special about the person. You can make an acrostic Valentine's Day card to let someone know why he or she is so special to you. Look at the examples on page 31 for help. When your poem is finished, you can decorate your card using colored paper, markers, and stickers.

DID YOU KNOW?

On Valentine's Day, make everyone around you feel special! Bring enough Valentine's Day cards for all your classmates so no one feels left out.

S-shares toys with me
A-always smiling
R-really good at basketball
A-a kind friend

C-cares about others
A-awesome skateboarder
R-really fun to be around
L-loyal to friends
O-only person I know that can juggle
S-shares his video games with me

Glossary

ancient Something related to a period of time long ago

community The people living in an area and the area itself

federal Decided by the government

festival A time of celebration in honor of a special occasion

loyalty Being faithful and true to someone

puzzik A type of card where the message is in a folded piece of paper

rebus A puzzle where words and pictures are used to write a message

retirement home A place where older people live when they need help caring for themselves

symbol Something that stands for something else

tradition A custom or belief handed down from one generation to another

virtual Something found on a computer

Index

balloons 17

cards 8, 12–15, 17, 23, 25, 27, 30

chocolates 22, 28

Cupid 18–19

decorations 16, 17, 22, 24, 25, 29, 30

flowers 22, 29

gifts 17, 22, 23

hearts 16–17, 19, 22, 23, 24, 29, 30

love 4, 5, 9, 16, 18, 19, 20, 21, 22, 26, 29

lovebirds 20–21

Lupercalia 6–7

mailboxes 25

parties 24

poems 30–31

Rome (Romans) 6, 7, 8, 10–11, 18

Saint Valentine 8–9

school 4, 24, 25, 30

strawberries 24, 28

traditions 10

Printed in China—CT